Getting into Golf

Ron Thomas and Joe Herran

CHELSEA HOUSE
PUBLISHERS

A Haights Cross Communications Company ®

Philadelphia

This edition first published in 2006 in the United States of America by Chelsea House Publishers, a subsidiary of Haights Cross Communications.

A Haights Cross Communications Company®

Chelsea House Publishers
2080 Cabot Blvd West, Suite 201
Langhorne, PA 19047-1813

The Chelsea House world wide web address is www.chelseahouse.com

First published in 2005 by
MACMILLAN EDUCATION AUSTRALIA PTY LTD
627 Chapel Street, South Yarra 3141

Visit our website at www.macmillan.com.au

Associated companies and representatives throughout the world.

Copyright © Ron Thomas and Joe Herran 2005

Library of Congress Cataloguing-in-Publication Data Applied for.
ISBN 0 7910 8811 1

Edited by Helena Newton
Text and cover design by Cristina Neri, Canary Graphic Design
Illustrations by Nives Porcellato and Andy Craig
Photo research by Legend Images

Printed in China

Acknowledgments
The authors wish to acknowledge and thank Jan Hipgrave, Judy Pitman and Barbara Gunn for their assistance and advice in the writing of this book.

The authors and the publisher are grateful to the following for permission to reproduce copyright material:

Cover photographs: Golf ball courtesy of Photodisc, and player courtesy of Picture Media/REUTERS/ Tim Shaffer.

Australian Picture Library, p. 27; IOC/Olympic Museum Collections, p. 30; Photodisc, pp. 1, 5, 6 (top and bottom); Photolibrary.com/AgeFoto, p. 9; Picture Media/REUTERS/Shaun Best, p. 23; Picture Media/REUTERS/Mike Blake, p. 25; Picture Media/REUTERS/Christian Charisius, p. 29; Picture Media/ REUTERS/Kevin Lamarque, p. 26; Picture Media/REUTERS/Jeff J Mitchell, p. 22; Picture Media/ REUTERS/Ellen Ozier, p. 4; Picture Media/REUTERS/Tim Shaffer, p. 7; Picture Media/REUTERS/Darren Staples, p. 28; Picture Media/REUTERS/Jeff Topping, p. 24.

Contents

Glossary words

When a word is printed in **bold**, you can look up its meaning in the Glossary on page 31.

The game

Golf is a popular game for men and women, boys, and girls in countries around the world. There are local golf clubs where people play for fun or in club tournaments. Some schools include golf for sport and golf schools teach people of all ages the skills of the game. Professional golfers travel the world playing for prize money at international competitions. Millions of fans watch these top players on television.

The history of golf

When golf began in Scotland in the 1400s, players hit stones, not balls. There were similar games in Europe but the Scots came up with the idea of hitting an object into a hole. The game spread around the world and now there are golf clubs and golf tournaments held almost everywhere. In Australia, golf was first played by Scottish migrants in the 1820s. The first Australian golf course was built in Tasmania in 1839.

Did you know?

In 1457, King James II banned golf in Scotland. He thought that archery was a better sport because it would help Scotland defend itself in battles against England.

Professional golfer Vijay Singh playing in the Wachovia Championship in North Carolina in 2004

Playing a round

A round of golf is played on a golf course that has nine or 18 **holes**. The player hits a ball into the holes using golf clubs. The player aims to complete the course taking as few hits, called strokes, as possible.

Players hit off from an area known as the **tee** or teeing ground. Up to four players can play together. Each player hits a ball down a long stretch of grass, called the fairway, to the green. The green is usually a smooth, mowed area of grass. The hole is in the green.

Once each player has hit the ball into the hole, all players move off to the next tee and hit off again. The player who takes the least number of strokes to complete the course is the winner. Players of average ability take about three and a half to four hours to complete 18 holes of golf.

A round of golf begins on an area called the tee or teeing ground.

Rule

Players are not allowed to carry more than 14 clubs at a time.

Equipment

Golfers carry clubs, balls, and tees in a golf bag, which can also be wheeled on a buggy. Some golfers ride around the course in a motorized golf cart.

A range of golf clubs

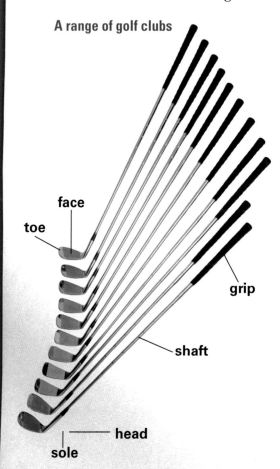

face

toe

grip

shaft

head

sole

A golf ball and tees

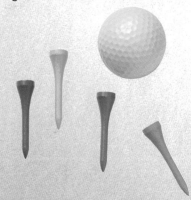

Clubs

A golf professional can help the player choose clubs with the right **grip**, length, weight, and flex. Club **shafts** are usually made of metal, or a metal-like substance called graphite. Grips are usually rubber. Head covers protect the clubs. Clubs kept clean and dry will last a long time.

There are four types of clubs: **irons**, **woods**, **wedges**, and the **putter**. Most of the clubs have stainless steel heads. Irons have heads that are set on an angle, known as **loft**. Irons are numbered depending on the angle. The higher the number, the larger the angle and the higher the ball will travel. Irons are used to hit the ball shorter distances. Woods are used to drive the ball long distances. The **driver** is one of the woods. Wedges are used to hit the ball out of sand bunkers or over grass around the green. Putters have flat heads. They are used on the green to **putt** the ball into the hole.

Balls and tees

Golf balls are small, hard, white, and dimpled. They measure 1.68 inches (4.26 centimeters) across. The ball is balanced on a wooden or plastic tee, which raises it off the ground while the player "tees off" at the start of a hole.

Clothing

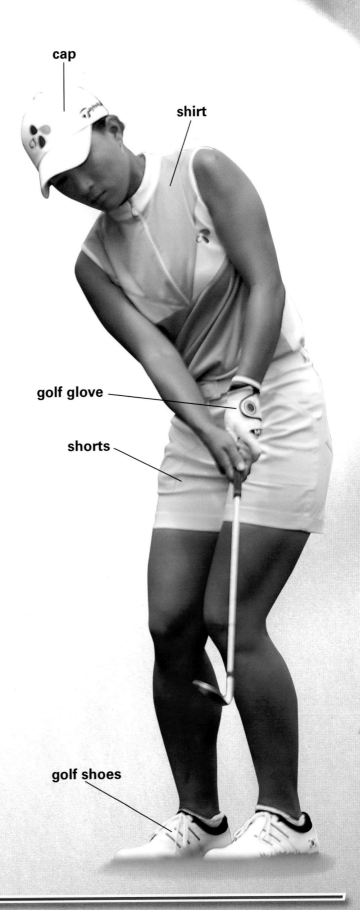

Many golf clubs have a "dress code" that requires players to wear only certain kinds of clothes, such as a collared shirt and trousers for men, and a shirt and skirt for women. Other golf clubs are less strict and allow players to wear shorts and shirts. Golfing clothes need to be comfortable. Golfers also wear a sunhat and carry an umbrella and waterproof jacket in case of rain.

Golf glove

A golf glove is sometimes worn on one hand so that the player can get a better grip on the club. A golf glove needs to fit securely.

Golf shoes

Golf shoes have rubber studs or spikes in the soles for a better grip on the grassy course.

cap

shirt

golf glove

shorts

golf shoes

The course

A golf course can have nine or 18 holes. An 18-hole golf course that is about 3.9 miles (6.2 kilometers) long takes a good player about 72 strokes to complete. The number of strokes that it is supposed to take to complete a hole or course is known as **par**. Golfers hit off from the tee or teeing ground. Fairways are the mowed grass areas between each tee and the green. The greens have the shortest grass on the course, although some greens are sand. The hole is on the green and is marked with a **flagstick**. The rough is the area outside the fairways consisting of long grass, bush, and trees. It is harder to hit the ball out of the rough than along the smooth fairway.

Hazards

Golf courses also contain **hazards** to make the course more difficult. A golfer might accidentally hit the ball into the hazards. It takes more strokes to get the ball out of these areas and back onto the fairway or the green. The two main hazards are:

- bunkers, which are hollow, sandy areas
- water hazards, such as ponds, streams, lakes, or other bodies of water.

A four-par hole

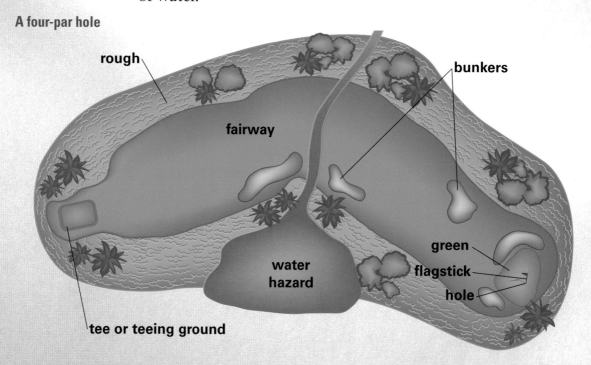

rough

bunkers

fairway

green

flagstick

hole

water hazard

tee or teeing ground

Players' behavior code

So that all golfers can enjoy the game of golf, players follow a code of behavior on the course. This code encourages players to care for others and for the course. Some of the rules of this code are:

All clubs, bags, and buggies must be left off the edge of the green.

- when taking a practice swing or playing a stroke, make sure that no one is standing nearby in a place where they may be hit by the club or the ball
- stand well back when another player is playing a stroke
- never talk or move while another player is about to play a stroke
- play without delay but not until the group ahead is out of range
- walk quickly between shots
- leave the green immediately after the hole has been played
- replace all **divots**, or fill in any holes made, with sand from a bucket
- when searching for a lost ball, allow the group behind to play past while the search continues
- rake or smooth over the sand in a bunker after a stroke has been played
- remove and replace the flagstick carefully on the green
- walk carefully on the green
- call out **"fore"** if a ball is hit toward other players.

Rule
Golfers are allowed to take practice swings on the teeing ground but cannot practice their strokes once a round has begun.

Skills

Beginning players learn the basic skills of golf, such as how to grip the clubs, how to **address** the ball and play different shots, how to choose the right club for various shots, and how to putt. They also learn how to avoid the hazards on the course and how to get out of them if a shot goes astray. With practice, players will develop these skills and improve their performance.

Gripping the club

Gripping or holding the club correctly is important if the player is going to hit the ball straight. The club is held so that the clubface is face-on to the ball. To get the correct grip on the club, the right-handed player follows these steps.

Gripping the club

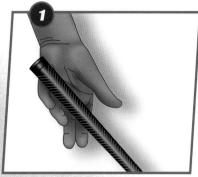

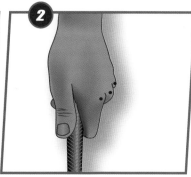

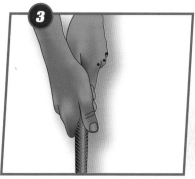

1 The club is placed in the left hand.

2 Looking down, the player sees two-and-a half knuckles of the left hand.

3 The player places the right hand below the left. The thumbs and forefingers point in the same direction and form V shapes.

Grips

These are the three main grips used by golfers.

The Vardon grip

The ten-finger or "baseball" grip

The interlocking grip

Addressing the ball

Addressing the ball is how players get their bodies into position to hit the ball. If the player adopts the correct stance and posture, the club will travel on the proper arc, and the ball will travel toward the target.

Setting up for a shot

When setting up for a shot, the right-handed player follows these steps.

Setting up

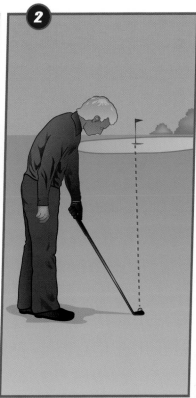

1 The player stands behind the ball and looks down an imaginary line to the target. Picking a mark about a yard in front of the ball, the player uses it to help visualize the imaginary line.

2 The player stands opposite the ball with the feet together. The player lines the club up behind the ball, keeping the legs straight and bending from the waist until the club touches the ground.

3 The player moves the feet about shoulder-width apart and bends the knees slightly. The weight is on the balls of the feet. The ball and the club's head are midway between the player's feet, although some players prefer to play the ball opposite the left foot. The shoulders, hips, knees, and feet are parallel to the target line and the clubface points at the target.

The swing

After forming a good grip and a good setup, comes the swing. The swing is a linked set of movements beginning with a slow backswing, followed by a smooth downswing, and finishing with the player following through, or turning to face the target.

Backswing

The backswing creates momentum or energy in the swing and sets the body and club in a position to complete a good shot.

The backswing

1 To start the backswing, the right-handed player's left hand and arm push the club back from the ball and the shoulders turn. The player keeps the head steady and over the ball.

2 When the club is at hip height, the toe of the club is pointing upward. The player's hips are turned away from the ball.

3 At the top of the backswing, the club is horizontal to the ground. The player's weight is on the right leg and the back is facing the target. The player's eyes are focused on the ball. The player is now ready for the downswing.

Downswing

There is only a split second between the end of the backswing and the beginning of the downswing. Right-handed players follow these steps for the downswing.

Did you know?

During a tournament in Melbourne in 1964, Arnold Palmer hooked a shot high into the fork of a gum tree. Palmer climbed 20 feet (6 meters) up the tree, turned his number 1 iron around, and knocked the ball 30 yards (24 meters) forward. He followed this with a chip shot to the green and then putted the ball into the hole.

The downswing

4 The player's hips turn as the left arm pulls the club down. The right knee is turning toward the target and most of the player's weight is on the left foot.

5 When the club hits the ball, the player's weight is on the left foot and the hips are turned fully to the left. The player's eyes are behind the ball and the heel of the right foot has lifted off the ground.

6 After impact, the through-swing turns the shoulders. The player's right knee bends in toward the target and the player follows through with the club and turns to watch the flight of the ball.

Using the clubs

Each hole starts with a tee shot. The player chooses a club that suits the length of the hole.

The driver

The driver is the club that hits the ball the farthest. However, not all players use the driver because it is a difficult club to use. Instead, they can choose another of the woods or irons. To use the driver or other woods, the right-handed player follows these steps.

Using the driver or woods

1 The player positions the ball opposite the left heel and stands with the feet shoulder-width apart. The top of the driver is in line with the center of the ball.

2 The player uses a smooth swing that sweeps the ball up and forward. The player keeps his or her balance by trying not to hit the ball too hard. The distance of this shot depends on timing, not on how hard the ball is hit.

3 The player follows through, watching where the ball is going.

Did you know?

According to the Guinness Book of Records 2004, *the record-holder of the longest golf ball drive is American Jack Hamm. On July 20, 1993, at Highland Ranch, Colorado, he drove a ball 458 yards (418.78 meters).*

Long irons, numbers 3 and 4

Long irons are used on the fairway shots. The player places the ball toward the center of the stance and the club head is low to the ground during the backswing. The player sweeps the ball off the grass with an unhurried swing.

Medium irons, numbers 5, 6, and 7

Medium irons hit the ball higher but nor as far as long irons. When using a medium iron, the right-handed player follows these steps.

Using a medium iron

1 The player positions the ball just left of center.

2 The player looks at the ball during the backswing.

3 The player swings down and through to hit the ball.

Short irons, numbers 8 and 9

Short irons lift the ball high into the air over shorter distances. When holding a short iron, the player's hands overlap more than for other clubs. When using a short iron, the right-handed player follows these steps.

Using a short iron

Woods and long irons hit the ball farther than all other clubs.

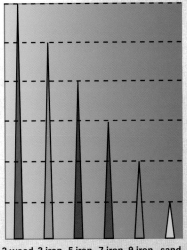

1 The player uses about three-quarters of the normal backswing.

2 On the downswing, the player's left hip is turned and the back of the ball is hit to make it rise.

3 wood 3 iron 5 iron 7 iron 9 iron sand wedge

The chip shot

A chip shot is a short, low shot played onto the green. The chip shot is used when the ball has not quite reached the green and when a player must get the ball over the rough grass and onto the green. The chip shot is usually played with a 6, 7, 8, or 9 iron or the pitching wedge. To perform a chip shot, the right-handed player follows these steps.

The chip shot

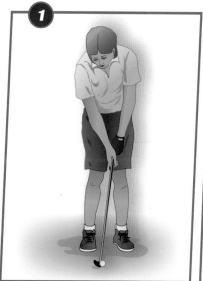

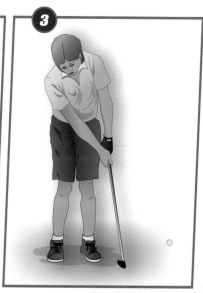

1 The player's feet are close together with the weight on the left foot. The hands are ahead of the ball, gripping a little way down the shaft of the club.

2 The sole of the club brushes the top of the grass before it hits the ball.

3 The player's eyes are still on the ground as the club hits and the ball is chipped up onto the green.

How a chip shot travels onto the green

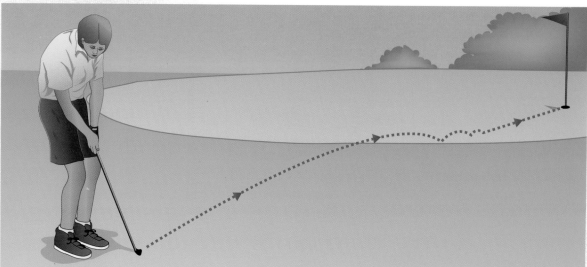

The pitch shot

The pitch shot is another short shot used to play onto the green. It is a high shot used to lift the ball into the air and onto the green. A pitching wedge is used for this shot. When performing a pitch shot, the right-handed player follows these steps.

The pitch shot

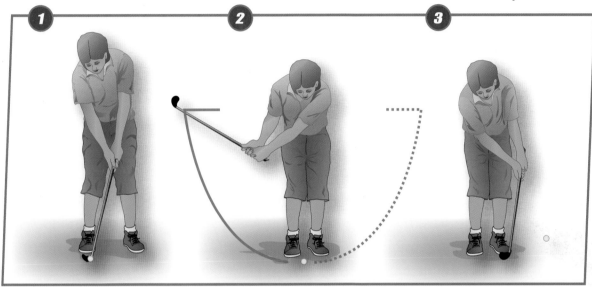

1 The player uses the club to move the ball into position in the middle of the stance.

2 The backswing is to about shoulder height. The player's arms and shoulders turn but the hips remain still.

3 The player's hands are ahead of the club's head when it hits the ball. The club ends up at the same height as the backswing— that is, at about shoulder height.

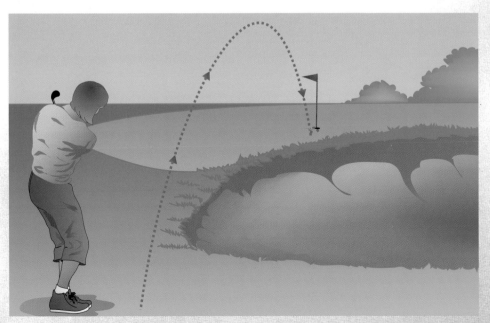

How a pitch shot travels up and onto the green

Putting

Once the ball is on the green, the putter is used to hit the ball into the hole. Players use a variety of different grips and styles when using the putter.

On the green, the player can mark the spot where the ball lies, remove the ball, and wait for his or her turn to putt. To mark the ball, the player places a marker behind the ball and, when it is time to play, the ball is replaced in front of the marker. This is done to ensure that the player does not hit a ball belonging to another player.

Preparing to putt

Before taking the shot, the player crouches behind the ball and looks along the path that the ball will travel to the hole. The player notices the way the grass is growing and how it slopes, and looks for any rough patches that might affect how the ball will roll to the hole.

The player can use the putter to help visualize the line between the ball and the hole before putting.

▮Rule▮

If the player plays a stroke with the wrong ball, two penalty strokes are added to the player's score.

Basic putting stroke

A good basic putting stroke is smooth, short, and low to the ground. The player uses a reverse-overlap grip so that all the fingers of the right hand are placed on the grip and the left forefinger is straight down over the top of the fingers of the right hand. When putting, the player follows these steps.

Putting

The reverse-overlap grip

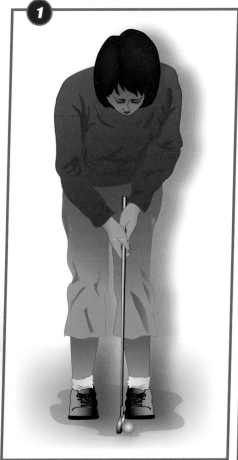

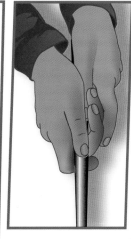

1 The player addresses the ball with the hands parallel to the putter. The player's head is directly over the ball and the player looks down.

2 The player hits the ball with very little movement of the body and swings the arms and shoulders like a pendulum, keeping the wrists firm.

Rules

Before taking the stroke, the player may decide to have the flagstick removed or held up above the hole.

A ball that comes to rest against the flagstick is said to be in the hole if it drops into the cup when the flagstick is removed.

Playing the hazards

Some of the hazards on a golf course are waterways and sand bunkers. Every golfer will hit the ball into one of these sooner or later. Golfers may also hit the ball into the rough on the edge of the fairway. Players must learn how to get out of these hazards, taking as few shots as possible.

Sand wedge

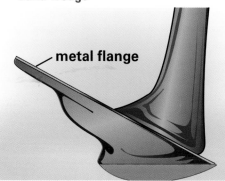

metal flange

Basic bunker shot

The basic bunker shot is used to hit the ball out of sand using a special club called the sand wedge. The sand wedge has a metal flange on the sole to enable the club to skid or "splash" under the ball.

After hitting the ball into a bunker, the player enters the sand behind the ball, making sure that the club does not touch the sand. Then the player twists the feet into the sand for a good foothold and grips a little way down the club. To perform a basic bunker shot, the right-handed player follows these steps.

▌Rule▌

Loose objects such as leaves and stones cannot be removed from a bunker.

The basic bunker shot

1 The player places the weight on the left foot so that the body faces to the left of the target.

2 The player does not turn the body very much during the backswing.

3 The club is swung through and hits the sand about 2 inches (5 centimeters) behind the ball, lifting it out on a cushion of sand.

Shots from the rough

A shot that goes off the fairway will land in the rough. The rough consists of rough grass, bush, and trees. A shot is needed to get the ball back onto the fairway or onto the green. To play a shot from the rough, the right-handed player follows these steps.

1 The player addresses the ball back toward the right foot, with the weight on the left foot.

2 The player takes only a three-quarter-length backswing.

3 The player swings down steeply behind the ball to pop it out of the grass. There is little or no follow-through on this shot.

Rules

The USGA (United States Golf Association) and the Royal and Ancient Golf Club of St. Andrews, Scotland, are joint authors of the rules of golf. The USGA is responsible for the rules in the United States and Mexico, and the Royal and Ancient Golf Club of St. Andrews is in charge of golf rules for the rest of the world. These organizations are responsible for making the rules of golf and for any changes to the rules.

Players need to learn and understand the basic rules before they are ready to play golf.

The Royal and Ancient Golf Club of St. Andrews, Scotland, is known as the home of golf.

On the tee

Players must follow certain rules while on the tee. These are:

- golfers cannot carry more than 14 clubs
- the hole must be played from the teeing ground; the player is not allowed to play in front of the teeing ground, which is two club lengths deep
- the player is allowed to put the ball back without any penalty if the ball falls off the tee.

Out of bounds

Every golf course has boundaries around the edges, which are clearly marked. If a ball goes out of bounds, the player must replay the shot from the same place as the original shot. A penalty stroke is added to the player's score.

Obstructions and impediments

Obstructions are human-made things on and around the golf course. Immovable obstructions include telephone poles, electricity pylons, or anything else made by people that is firmly fixed to the ground. The player can move the ball away if his or her stance or swing will be affected. Movable obstructions include benches, lawn mowers, rakes, and hoses. These can be moved, but a penalty stroke is added to the player's score if the ball is accidentally moved while the obstruction is being moved.

Impediments are natural things in the environment such as leaves, stones, or twigs. They may be removed before playing the shot. However, if the ball is moved as the player touches any impediment, a penalty stroke is added to the player's score.

Unplayable ball

The player may declare that the ball is not playable. When this happens the player has one of three choices:

1 Replay the shot from where the ball was originally and add a penalty stroke.

2 Drop the ball within two club lengths of the spot where it is but no nearer to the hole and add a penalty stroke.

3 Move the ball back as far as the player likes and drop it there, adding one penalty stroke.

The player may choose to drop the ball within two club lengths of the place it landed if the ball is unplayable.

Scoring

Each hole on a golf course is given a par number. Par is the number of strokes it is supposed to take for a good player to get the ball from the tee to the hole. When the par numbers for each of the 18 holes are added together, the par for the course is the result. The possible scores for a hole are:

- par, when the player hits the ball into the hole with the number of strokes for the hole or par
- a birdie, when the player hits the ball into the hole in one stroke less than par; for example, a par-four hole in three strokes
- an eagle, when the player hits the ball into the hole in two strokes less than par; for example, a par-five hole in three strokes
- an albatross, when the player hits the ball into the hole in three strokes less than par; for example, a par-five hole in two strokes
- a bogey, when the player hits the ball into the hole in one stroke more than par; for example, a par-three hole in four strokes
- a double bogey, when the player hits the ball into the hole in two strokes more than par; for example, a par-three hole in five strokes
- a triple bogey, when the player hits the ball into the hole in three strokes more than par; for example, a par-three hole in six strokes
- a hole in one, when the player hits the ball into the hole in one stroke. This is very rare.

Scores for each player are recorded on a scorecard at the completion of each hole.

There are two main ways of scoring a game of golf:

1 Matchplay, in which the player who wins the greater number of holes wins.
2 Strokeplay, in which the player taking the lowest number of strokes for the course wins.

Officials

The number of officials at a tournament depends on the size of the golf event and whether the event is for amateur or professional players.

For an amateur golf event involving up to 200 players, the officials are:

- two starters, one for the first tee and one for the tenth tee, who start the field of players
- two scorers who check and collate the scores at the end of the tournament; the scorers display the results on a scoreboard and also record them using a laptop computer
- four rules officials for both the morning and afternoon. Rules officials monitor play and answer questions about rules. They also ensure that players do not delay play unnecessarily.

Players can call on officials to answer questions about rules.

For bigger events, many more officials are required. Officials for bigger events include:

- marshals who control spectators
- 52 rules officials, one for each player group who, as well as answering questions about rules, radio progressive scores back to the media center for live scoring on the Internet
- six media center workers
- three two-member teams for leaderboards, on which a hole-by-hole score of the ten best golfers is posted
- caddies, who are the people who carry clubs for the players.

Rule

The player may have only one caddy at any one time. If a player's caddy breaks any rule, the player suffers the penalty!

Player fitness

Golfers need to be fit if they are to perform to the best of their ability. Running, swimming, and cycling build stamina and fitness.

Warming up and stretching

Before a game or a practice session, it is important for golfers to warm up all their muscles by stretching them. Stretching helps make players more flexible and helps the muscles and joints move more easily. It also helps prevent injuries such as muscle tears, strains, and joint injuries.

Neck stretches

The player tilts the head forward and slowly rolls the head to one shoulder and then the other. These exercises help prevent stiffness in the neck and keep the neck flexible.

Side stretches

The player raises the right hand above the head and slowly leans to the left. The stretch is then repeated, raising the left hand above the head and leaning slowly to the right.

Stretching exercises, such as the hamstring stretch, are done in an easy and relaxed way and each position is held for at least 10 seconds.

Calf stretches

The player places one foot in front of the other and leans forward, but keeps the back heel on the ground. The player pushes forward until the calf muscle in the back leg stretches. The stretch is repeated for the other leg.

Thigh stretches

Standing on one leg, the player holds the ankle of the raised leg. The player pulls the foot back to stretch the thigh, keeping the knees close together. The player can lean against a wall or hold onto another player for balance. The stretch is then repeated for the other leg.

Hamstring stretches

The player sits on the ground with the legs extended in front of the body and the knees straight. The player bends forward slowly and reaches toward the toes. Hamstring stretches can be performed by placing one foot on the golf bag with the knee raised up.

Back stretch

Holding a club behind the head and across the shoulders, the player twists the body to the right, lifting the left heel off the ground. The stretch is repeated, twisting the body to the left and lifting the right heel off the ground.

Golfers perform stretches, such as the back stretch using a club, to prevent injuries.

Competition

The Professional Golfers' Association (PGA) of the United States is one of the largest sports organizations in the world, with more than 27,000 members. The association conducts 40 tournaments each year and four of them—the PGA Championship, Senior PGA Championship, Ryder Cup Matches, and PGA Grand Slam of Golf—are among the most important golf tournaments in the world. The PGA Grand Slam of Golf is a match exclusively for the winners of some of golf's other major tournaments, including the Masters, the British Open, the U.S. Open, and the PGA Championships.

The 2003 British Open was won by Ben Curtis of the United States.

The British Open

The oldest and the most famous of the world tournaments is the British Open. The Royal and Ancient Golf Club of St. Andrews, which runs major championships for both professional and amateur golfers, organizes the British Open. Since 2001, there has also been a Women's British Open.

Did you know?

The first British Open Championship for golf was played in 1860 and the prize was a red leather belt with a silver buckle.

PGA Tour

In the United States, an organization called the PGA Tour runs competitions for top male professional golfers as well as a Ladies Professional Golf Association Tour. A tour is a series of professional competitions that moves from one golf course to another, week after week.

There is also a PGA European Tour. This tour covers countries in Europe and is another important professional golf tour.

Solheim Cup

The Solheim Cup is a contest between teams of professional women golfers from Europe and the United States. The first Solheim Cup match was played in 1990 and it is now played every two years. The competition is named after Karsten Solheim, the founder of a golf equipment company.

The European team won the Solheim Cup in Sweden in September 2003.

Ryder Cup

The Ryder Cup is a contest between teams of top professional men golfers from Europe and the United States. The first Ryder Cup match was played in 1927. It is now played every two years. The competition is named after Samuel Ryder, a businessman who donated the trophy for the first Ryder Cup.

Olympic golf

Golf was an Olympic event for both men and women in 1900 in Paris, France. Men played a tournament over 72 holes while women played nine holes.

At the St. Louis Olympic Games in 1904, there was no women's golf tournament but men had a tournament for individual players and for ten-man teams. All of the competitors were from the United States except for Canadian George Lyon, who won the individual championship.

Olympic women's golf was last played in 1900 in Paris, France.

Golf has not been included in the Olympic Games since that time. The International Olympic Committee (IOC) is considering whether to include golf for the Beijing Olympic Games in 2008.

Did you know?

Snow golf was invented by English author Rudyard Kipling when he was living in Vermont in the 1890s. He painted his golf balls red so that they could be located in the snow.

Glossary

address	take the position in preparation to play a stroke
divots	pieces of grass taken out of the ground when striking the ball
driver	the golf club that hits the ball the farthest; the driver is one of the woods
flagstick	a movable pole with a flag attached, which shows the position of the hole
fore	a warning shouted to tell other players that a ball is approaching them
grip	the handle of a golf club
hazards	areas of the course where a golfer might accidentally hit the ball, which are difficult to get the ball out of, such as bunkers or water obstacles
holes	4.3-inch holes cut into the putting greens with cups inside them, which golfers aim to hit the ball into
irons	golf clubs with metal heads and sloped faces, which are used to hit the ball shorter distances
loft	the slope of the clubface; also, the action of hitting the ball into the air
par	the number of strokes it is supposed to take to play a hole or course
putt	to hit the ball gently so that it rolls along the green and into the hole
putter	a golf club with a short, stiff shaft used for putting on the green
shafts	long stems attached to the heads of golf clubs
tee	the area where golfers hit off at the start of a hole; also, the small plastic or wooden object that is driven into the ground for a golf ball to sit on
wedges	golf clubs used to hit balls out of bunkers or over the fringe of grass around the green
woods	golf clubs with heads made of wood, stainless steel, or a material called titanium, which are used to hit the ball longer distances

Index